Puppet Making

This edition published 1978 by
Wayland (Publishers) Limited
49 Lansdowne Place, Hove, East Sussex BN3 1HF

SBN 85340 620 0

Filmset by Filmtype Services Limited, Scarborough
Printed in Italy by New Interlitho SpA

Beginning Crafts Series
Created and produced by Sackett Publishing Services Ltd
2 Great Marlborough Street London W1

Photography by Robert Glover Studios, Amersham, Bucks

Beginning Crafts

Puppet Making

Stuart & Patricia Robinson

Illustrated by Patricia Capon

Wayland Publishers England

Contents

Introduction to puppet making

Puppetry as an art goes back thousands of years. According to tradition, it was common in India in about 2000 BC. It is known also to have been popular in ancient China and other parts of Asia.

The stories were about legendary heroes and gods, and were set to music and performed on open-air stages. These were made from bamboo poles that were easy to move and put up when needed. They were used for shadow puppets, rod puppets, and marionettes.

The Greeks, Romans, and early Christians used puppets in their religious plays. After the decline of the Roman Empire the puppeteers spread through Europe giving their shows at festivals, market places, and the courts of the nobility. The State and Church condemned some of the shows as 'blasphemous, unclean, and not fit for children and females'. They called the puppeteers rogues and vagabonds. By the 1400s they were the star turns of the noisy amusements at the great trading fairs held around Europe.

From then on puppets were particularly popular in England. Showmen travelled from Italy and France to perform. Samuel Pepys says in his diary that he was pleased mightily when he took his wife to see Polichinello at Moorfields.

Punch arrived in England from Italy in the 1660s, where he was known as Pulcinella, a character in the *commedia dell'arte* plays. He first became the Punch we know in the galanty show at Bartholomew Fair in 1703. His wife, Joan, did not become Judy until 1818. These characters developed as popular glove puppets during the 1880s. The galanty shows travelled the country, showing Punch and Judy during the day and shadow puppets at night.

Shadow puppets had started in India or China with large, highly coloured, flat-hinged, part cut-out paper 'shadows' with wire faces. They arrived in Europe in the late 1600s and were known as Ombres Chinois.

Peepshows had grown out of the perspective boxes of the 1400s. Some were vast panoramas, while others were tiny enough to be set in eggs or the handles of quill pens.

The showmen had by now acquired large horse-drawn caravans fitted out with the luxuries of a wealthy man's house. The showmen travelled all over the British Isles, and many crossed the Channel to tour Europe.

The spread of the cinema from the early 1900s greatly affected the growth of puppetry, which did not really recover until after World War I.

Many puppet theatres were begun in European cities, but the wandering puppeteer did not really come back until after World War II.

Marionettes and rod puppets are also of ancient origin. The marionette needs more skill than the glove puppet, as the operator is one stage further removed from the puppet.

Many marionettes were a metre or more in height. Some needed several operators and were able to perform elaborate tricks. They smoked cigarettes and pipes, drank from glasses, played the piano, and danced. Rod puppets are much more limited in control than other puppets, but still very effective.

One of the latest developments is the ventriloquist's doll. These puppets are usually operated by one hand in the back of the body. This works bars or strings that open and shut the lower mouth, move the head and eyes, and sometimes the legs. Some of the popular film and television puppets, such as the Muppets, are based on this technique.

Art of puppetry

With the simplest of materials, you can make all the puppets in this book. None of them is difficult to make and you will probably find almost everything you need either at home or at school.

You need scraps of material left over from dressmaking. You will also need all kinds of kitchen rubbish, boxes, cartons, plastic bottles, and so on. Scraps of wood, paints, and felt-tipped pens are needed, and very ordinary tools such as a craft knife, scissors, and, for some of the puppets, a hammer and a tenon saw. With these materials and tools you can start on one of the most fascinating art crafts in the world, puppetry.

Making the puppets will give you many hours of pleasure and a lot of fun. Once you have made a puppet which is all your own, you will want to give it life, to make it move and talk. As soon as your first glove puppet is on your hand, it becomes like a person with a character. It even has a special voice. Try it for yourself. You will see immediately that a voice for the puppet comes naturally to you.

The more you practise with a puppet the better you will become at handling it. Use a mirror so that you can watch your own actions. You could place a mirror in such a way that you could look into it and operate the puppet over the edge of a table without being seen yourself. It helps the effect if you arrange a desk lamp so that the puppet is spotlighted.

You can make puppets do anything you like. You can make them laugh, cry, get angry, or be sad. All you have to do is to alter the angle of the head and the way you work the arms. You can make them talk to the audience and ask the audience to reply. You can tell jokes, ask riddles, sing songs, talk to other puppets. Your audience will be captivated. You only have to watch people while they are at a puppet show. They are completely taken up by what is happening on stage. You will find that the audience likes to help the puppet to find things, and to warn him when he is in danger. They will sing with him, and they love it when the puppet talks to one of the audience, calling him by name. Then they feel that they really are part of the show. The fact that they know someone is operating the glove or pulling the marionette's strings doesn't spoil any of the fun. They know the voice that is talking to them is human. The magic lies in the art of puppetry, which is as real and believable as the live theatre itself.

Putting on a show There is a lot of fun and excitement to be had out of putting on your own puppet show. You can do it alone or with a friend, or a group of friends can get together. You can write a script and have proper readings and rehearsals for voices. Or you can work without a script, making the plot up as you go. It is best to have a basic idea to begin with. Some puppeteers find that this is the best way. The puppets themselves will help you to know what to make them say.

Puppet stages and theatres Puppeteers use all kinds of stages and theatres. Some are quite wonderful and are just like miniature theatres with wings, stage, backdrops, scenery, lighting systems, and music. Puppeteers who travel with their shows usually work with a lightweight, box-shaped frame, which is covered with fabric. The Punch and Judy show that you see on the beach is made this way. This can be put up and taken down again very quickly and it is usually light to carry. Some puppeteers have a three-panelled wooden screen, which opens and stands up. The centre panel has a hole in it for a stage and the curtains push back on rails to the sides. You may not want to go to all the trouble of making a puppet theatre at first. You can make improvised theatres and stages in different ways.

Improvised theatres The obvious makeshift theatre is a big cardboard box set on a table. The table must be covered with a dark table cloth, right down to the floor on all sides. The puppeteers work from behind the table. Cut one side of the box away for a stage front. Cut about half of the base away. This part overhangs the back of the table, where the puppeteers are working. Lay a heavy stick or kitchen weights along the front of the stage to balance the box on the table. You can paint scenery on the inside of the box, or line it first with white paper and then paste on paper cut-outs to represent scenery. You can also paint the front of the box for the proscenium (front of stage). You can even make curtains if you like. If the box seems a bit flimsy after you have cut away the side and part of the base, strengthen the inside of the box with panels cut from other boxes. Glue the pieces in position.

For a different kind of improvised theatre you will need two tables, one a little smaller than the other. Stand the smaller table on top of the larger. The larger table should have a dark cloth draped over it as before. Drape another cloth over the top and sides of the smaller table, leaving the front facing the audience open. Work between the tables and the wall, sitting on a low stool or a bench.

A wooden clothes dryer that folds in three makes a good theatre too. Pin paper or fabric over each side to cover the spaces. Leave just the middle top space open for a stage.

A doorway also makes a good stage. Wedge a stick across the open doorway. Pin a piece of cloth across the doorway below the stick. (The stick is to give the puppets something to work against.) If the room behind the stage is in darkness, the effect of this improvised theatre is very convincing.

Lights and music You need lighting to give a realistic theatrical atmosphere. Angled desk lamps are useful. Set two or three behind the audience, directed towards the stage. Or, set them in front of the stage on the floor, the lamps directed upwards to the stage. If you have a tape recorder you can put music on tape for an opening mood setter. If your play needs sound effects, put these on tape too. Music can sometimes add just the atmosphere you want during the play. The handkerchief ghost puppets on pages 42–43 are fun if you just work them against a plain background in full light. But if you paint a set with a graveyard and a full moon, and play some spooky music, you will have the audience shivering as the ghosts glide about the stage.

A typical Javanese shadow puppet

TECHNIQUE AND PROJECT

Shadow puppets

Shadow puppets are one of the oldest forms of puppetry and the most easily operated. Shapes cut out of paper are moved against a transparent screen. The puppeteer has the light behind him, and the audience watch moving shadows on their side of the screen. Shadow shows can be silent or you can play background music.

Materials, tools, and equipment
A rectangular picture frame
Covering for the frame (thin cotton, nylon, silk, etc.) 100 mm larger all round than the frame

2 G-clamps (for fixing the frame to the table)
Tacks, hammer, wire cutters
Black paper, scissors, 15-gauge wire
Adhesive tape

Method Fold in the edges of the fabric 25 mm all round **(1)**. Spread the fabric over the frame **(2)**. Tap in one tack at the middle of a side through the doubled fabric (marked 1 on the diagram). Put one tack in the middle of the other three sides **(4)**. Continue putting tacks in either side of the central tacks, pulling the fabric taut as you work **(3)**. The fabric should be like a drum when you have finished.

The shadow puppet Cut out a figure in stiff black paper. Pierce holes for the eyes **(5)**. Make a control rod for the puppet. This can be a piece of wire, a thin wooden rod, or even a tube of rolled-up paper **(6)**. Tape the control rod to the back of the puppet. If you

want a lot of characters in your shadow play you could glue a small strip of 'stick-and-touch' fastening (used in dressmaking) to the back of the puppets and another piece on the end of the rod. Then you can simply pull the rod from the puppet and quickly pick up and fasten on another.

Setting up the screen Fix the G-clamps to the inside edge of the frame and to the edge of the table top. If you prefer, you can support the frame between piles of books. Position a lamp behind you so that it shines onto the back of the screen. Place a mirror behind the audience so that you can watch the effect of the puppets in the mirror. If a puppet is held right against the screen the shadow will be clear and sharp. Hold it away from the screen and the image will be larger but fainter. Practise moving the puppets so that they move on and off the screen without jerking.

Shadow puppet scenery

When you have made your shadow screen and tried out your first shadow puppets you will find that they need some kind of set or scenery to make their actions seem real to the audience. The scenery should add to the story, but not get in the way of the puppets as they move across the screen. Scenery can be made of black paper, coloured cellophane or tissue paper. It can be fixed to the screen itself or attached to a separate sheet of acetate film to make scene-changing easier.

Method Draw the scenery on black paper with a piece of chalk. Make sure that you leave enough space for the puppets to move around in. Cut holes in the scenery **(1)**. If you can cut holes that open and shut like doors or windows, these add to the effect. Tape pieces of coloured tissue or cellophane behind the cut-out holes.

You can mark some of the scenic effects on the screen itself if you like **(2)**. Large pieces of coloured transparent paper or film can be used to cut out whole pieces of scenery.

If the scenery is complicated you may get shadows on the scenery edges. You can prevent this by cutting a piece of tracing paper or acetate film to the size of the screen. Pin this over the scenery so that you 'sandwich' the scenery between the screen and the covering film **(3)**.

Scenery can also be drawn or painted directly onto the back of the screen itself with inks or watercolours

(4). You can use felt-tipped pens, but the colour may run a bit and should only be used for big areas or bold effects.

If you make your shadow screen from cardboard rather than using a picture frame, you can make it with panels on both sides for 'wings'. Have a series of different stage sets ready to be lifted up and quickly taped to the back of the screen. If a cardboard shadow screen with wings is made in three pieces with the wings folded back, the screen will stand on the table without needing to be supported.

Wire-frame fish

Giant, wire-frame shadow puppets were used by the ancient Chinese, Japanese, and Javanese, sometimes in the performance of operas. This use of wire in making shadow puppets had an influence on many of the shadow puppet designs made at the famous Bauhaus School of Art and Design in Germany in the 1920s. Machinery made in wire outlines appeared to have cogwheels whirring round and hammers falling, and weird wire robots moved among the machinery. Sometimes, geometric shapes moved on the screens, acting out stories. Bad men triangles robbed fat little circles, and squares hopped after the triangles in pursuit.

Wire-frame puppets are fascinating to make and to work with. The light glows through the thin, coloured paper, making the shape look alive. If the shape is made in two pieces and each piece is operated on a separate rod, lifelike movement can be worked.

Materials, tools, and equipment
Self-adhesive film, wire cutters,
15-gauge wire, tissue paper,
coloured inks, cellophane

Method Draw and cut a paper pattern. Cut a piece of wire about 45 cm long. Bend it into the fish shape. Start with the tail. Bend a separate piece of wire to hold the tail in shape **(1)**. Cut a piece of transparent film, using the paper pattern of the fish. Cut it 12 mm bigger all round. Tear the paper back-

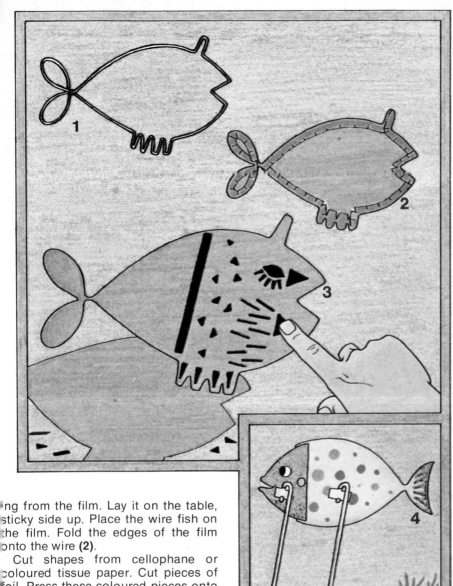

ng from the film. Lay it on the table, sticky side up. Place the wire fish on the film. Fold the edges of the film onto the wire **(2)**.

Cut shapes from cellophane or coloured tissue paper. Cut pieces of foil. Press these coloured pieces onto the sticky surface **(3)**. Cut another fish-shaped piece of adhesive film. Strip off the backing paper and place the film, sticky side down, over the decoration. You can add more decoration with felt-tipped pens or ink if you like. Tape a wire control rod to the back of the fish.

Dual control puppet Make the fish in two parts with a separate wire outline for the head and body. Bend a piece of stiff wire to make a control for each section. Tape the control rods to the fish **(4)**. The two parts can be operated with the edges just overlapping. You could join the two pieces either with a loop of wire, or a split pin.

Jointed shadow puppet

These shadow puppets can be shaped like people or animals and can be as simple or as complex as you like. Human figures can have separate control rods for each limb, and for the head and upper body. Animals can have control rods for the front and hind legs and also for the head. The figure in the photograph has been separated into parts so that you can see how the rider has been put together. The puppet has very few control rods. There are only three, one for the head and one for each pair of the horse's legs. The rest of the pieces are left swinging on the pinned joints, so that there is movement in the puppet as it is moved across the screen.

Materials, tools, and equipment
Stiff black card
15-gauge wire, wire pliers or cutters, hole punch
Push-through paper fasteners (split pins)
Adhesive tape, sharp craft knife, scrap paper, pencil

Method Draw your character on scrap paper first. It can be a single figure or two related characters such as a clown and his dog **(1)**. Mark on your rough drawing the points at which the figures might move, and the amount of overlap necessary between the parts **(2)**. You must always remember that you only have two hands with which to operate your puppet. You can have more than two

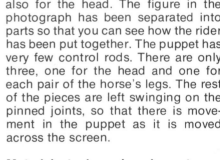

ontrol rods, but you have to support
he puppet while working the other
od.

Some of the joints will just swing
n the split pins, but try and make
ure that the important movements
n your characters are controlled by
he rods. You do not want uncon-
rolled movements, such as legs wav-
ng about, or arms dropping. Draw
ach of the separate parts on the
ardboard, allowing space between
hem **(3)**. Cut out each part carefully.
Punch small holes at the joints. Put in
split pin at each joint, not too tight-
y, but so that the joints have free
movement **(4)**.

Putting on control rods You usually
need one rigid support to hold the
figure and one rod attached to hands

or legs to control the movement of
the shadow **(5)**. You will probably
have to experiment a bit to decide the
best place to put the rods.

Choosing rods Rods can be made
of paper tubes or of wood. Wire usually makes the best rods because it is
strong enough to hold the figure and
thin enough not to cast too great a
shadow. Adhesive tape will hold a
wire rod to the back of the figure.
Bend the top of the rod and tape it
under. Fabric adhesive tape is useful
as it is the strongest tape.

Other techniques For a different
effect, try cutting some areas of the
shadow puppet away, and stick coloured tissue paper or film behind the
cut-out.

Hand shadow puppets

Once shadow puppets had become a form of entertainment it was not long before someone found that by putting their hands against a screen they could make animal, bird, or human shapes. From this, decorations were added to the hands, and hand shadows became an accepted form of puppetry.

Materials, tools, and equipment

Your hands and perhaps those of a
　friend
A shadow screen or a sheet hung
　across a doorway
A desk lamp with a bright bulb
For dressing up the hands – false
　hair, tissue paper, bits of fur, etc.

Method Make a screen first. This could be a shadow screen made of cardboard, standing on a table with the audience in front. Or it could be a white sheet pinned up across a doorway. The sheet should be as taut as possible, with no wrinkles. Make sure that no light glimmers through the sides of the sheet. Set up the lighting. For hand shadows, the light should come from behind and to the side. For full body shadows, set the light immediately behind. Simple hand shadows are the easiest to begin with. In the drawings you will see how to make a butterfly **(1)**, bird **(2)**, goose's head **(3)**, funny face **(4)**.

Hand shapes can be exaggerated by taping pieces of cellophane or pieces of tissue paper to the hand **(5)** and **(6)**. Or you can sew the pieces to a glove. This is a particularly effective trick when making animal shadows, such as prehistoric monsters, and so on. You can also use your head to

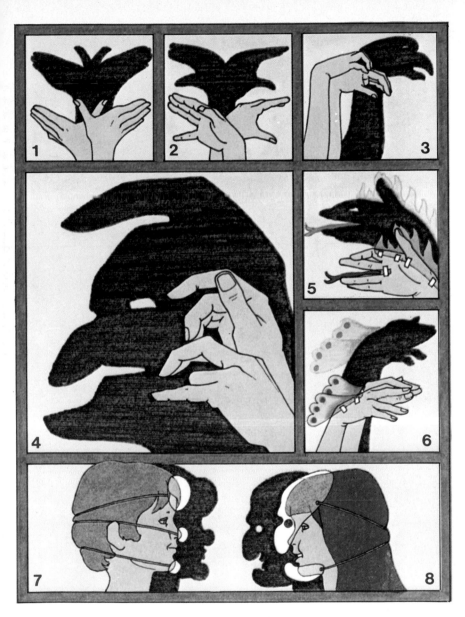

make a shadow puppet. Foam sponge pads can be fastened to the forehead, head, chin, or the nose, with rubber bands to distort the features and yet still allow you to speak and make facial movements **(7)** and **(8)**. If pieces are added to the ears, these will appear when the wearer turns his head to face the screen. You can also add details such as hair, moustaches, beards, long teeth, noses, extra-long fingers, big hands, and so on.

Hand shadows could be used together with cut-out paper shadows for certain stories. Peter and the Wolf for instance could have Peter as a cut-out, with the animals and birds as hand shadows. This would enable several performers to take part at once.

17

Paper bag puppets

One of the simplest forms of glove puppets is the paper bag puppet. In America, a group of actors called the Paper Bag Players use paper bags and boxes for all of their costumes and scenery.

Materials, tools, and equipment
Paper bags, large enough to fit on
    your hand (not plastic bags)
Scissors, watercolour paints, brushes,
    felt-tipped pens
Scraps for decorating puppets,
    beads, bits of lace, gold and silver
    foil, coloured tissue, feathers, etc.
Strong, clear adhesive

Method Try the elephant puppet first. Copy the shape illustrated onto thin, stiff cardboard **(1)**. Paint in the eyes. Cut the hole for the trunk **(2)**. To work the elephant puppet, put the middle finger through the hole for a trunk. Use three fingers and a thumb for legs to walk the puppet along **(3)**.

Make sure that the bag is deep enough to cover your hand completely and still have about a quarter of it free at the bottom to fold over **(4)**. This is the part which you decorate with felt-tipped pens or watercolour paints **(5)**. If you like, cut holes for eyes or for a mouth. Cut holes for fingers to come through at the sides and make arms **(6)**.

Use nylon doll's hair for hair, beard, or moustache effects. Make jewellery from gold or silver foil paper, or from beads.

To use the puppet, insert the hand into the bag and then bend it over at the top so that you are holding the bottom edge and the fold between thumb and fingers **(7)**. This helps you to move the bottom of the bag so that you can open and close the mouth.

You can also add a skirt to the bottom of the bag by stapling on a frill of crêpe or tissue paper. The skirt helps to hide the operator's arm **(8)**.

This type of puppet needs a proper stage of some kind, such as a cut-out cardboard box, for the best effect.

Large-sized paper bags and sacks can be made into body puppets. Paint the outsides with stripes, fur effects, etc., to make animals, and glue on paper ears so that the animal is identified. Cut slits in the sides of the bag for your arms to come through.

Instant glove puppets

Anyone can make an instant glove puppet, anywhere and at any time. You can make them to entertain young children, or on a journey when everyone else is getting rather bored or tired. All you need is your hand **(1)**, a handkerchief, and two or three rubber bands. Try it and see. You will be delighted with these hidden puppets.

They are always in your hands and ready to appear at any time.

Materials, tools, and equipment
Plain or patterned fabric, about 450 mm square
Rubber bands, card rolls, scraps of coloured paper, beads, feathers. pieces of junk jewellery, felt-tipped pens, watercolour paints, fabric paints, brushes

Method If you can obtain cardboard rolls, cut a ring to fit your first finger, about 37 mm long. (If you cannot obtain cardboard rolls, make a roll by rolling a piece of flexible cardboard, and tape the join.) Cover your hand with a piece of cloth **(2)**. Slide an elastic band over the card ring head and down to make a neck. Put elastic

bands on your first and fourth fingers to make arms (3). Leave plenty of the cloth hanging down, particularly in front. Use a felt-tipped pen to draw in features – eyes, nose, mouth, etc. You can now dress your puppet with necklaces of beads and a hat made from paper (4). He could be given a head of hair. Frayed string, raffia, cotton wool or an unravelled nylon pot scourer all make hair of a kind.

See if your puppet can pick things up. Perhaps he can put the things he finds in a small box. Give him some props to work with, a basket or a broom made of twigs or a bat for playing cricket. He could be a fighting puppet and wield a sword made of cardboard painted gold. You can develop the idea of an instant puppet by attaching paper or fabric cloaks to represent animals. Attach a cloak to the first finger with an elastic band and make a paper mask to fit over the head. Use your first two fingers for front paws (5). Make a monster. Make antennae from pipe cleaners or use glitter paint, or make tinsel or wool yarn feelers (6).

To perform with these puppets, either sit on the floor and rest the puppet on the table edge, or work through the back of an open chair frame.

21

Junk puppets

A puppet to be operated on the hand can be made from all kinds of things you might think were just rubbish. If you are going to take up puppet-making, start today to collect everything you can find that might make a puppet. Boxes, cans, yoghurt pots, washing-up liquid bottles, fibre flower pots, old balls, tights or stockings, mittens and socks, matchboxes, cotton reels, corks, and pieces of material and trimmings of all kinds. All these, and other things, will make very impressive puppets.

The two puppets illustrated are just ideas which you might like to try out. After that, you can try and make up your own puppets from the rubbish you have collected.

Method for making Sugar-box Joe
The first thing this puppet needs is a sock body. An old brown sock has been used. A sugarcube box is the next piece of junk. If you want to try and make him, here is how it is done.

Cut the bottom out of the sugar box. Tape the sock, with the foot cut

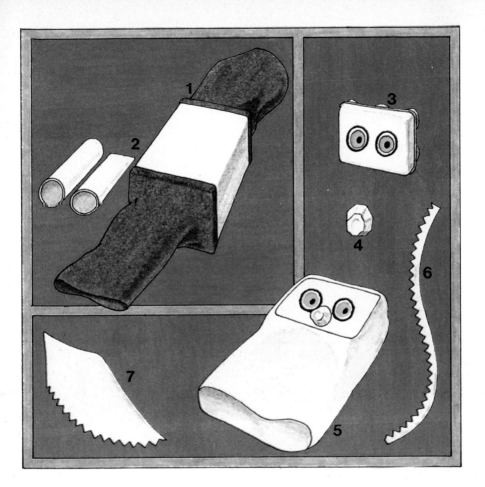

off, to the bottom edge of the box, stretching the cut edge. Tape the cut-off foot to the other end of the box for a hat **(1)**.

Flatten a cardboard tube (the box face illustrated has a tube from the inside of a roll of toilet paper). Glue the tube to the front of the head for a nose **(2)**. Cut out felt eyes, eyebrows, and hair. Cut two circles of card for big ears.

The beard is made from a scrap of kapok, but you could also use cotton wool or even wood or cellophane shavings.

Method for making Snowy Owl This is a charming puppet which you will love on sight. You need an empty egg carton, made of paper pulp, some paints, and some white fleecy fabric. Paint the egg box white. Cut out the bottoms of two indentations in the base to make eye sockets. Paint these orange with a black ring round **(3)**. Separate the two parts of the egg carton. Cut off one of the egg containers from the top and glue it to the bottom section for a beak. Paint a mouth in orange and black **(4)**. Cut a strip of the white fabric 45 cm long × 37 cm wide. Sew two short edges to make a tube. Glue one end of the tube around the edges of the egg carton **(5)**. Cut a strip with a jagged edge, and glue round the face **(6)**. Cut wing shapes **(7)** and sew to each side of the body. To operate, put the middle finger in the beak and the first and fourth fingers in the eyes.

Sock and mitten puppets

Sock and mitten puppets are another kind of junk puppet. They are made from old, cast-off clothing and cost very little to make. These puppets are similar to the glove puppet in the next project. All you need is a soft covering for your hand, flexible enough for you to make it appear to act and perform.

Materials, tools, and equipment
One striped sock, red felt
Pipe cleaners, black paint or ink
Beads for eyes, embroidery threads

Method for making Snake sock puppet Lay the sock flat on the table **(1)**. Cut a square of red felt, and also a rectangle. Round off the corners **(2)**. Glue or sew the pieces of felt to the sock as shown **(3)**.

When you put your hand in the sock you will find that you can open and shut the red mouth between thumb and fingers. With the sock on your hand, mark the position for the eyes and ears **(4)**. Cut two circles for the ears and sew them on. Sew on two button eyes. Make whiskers from

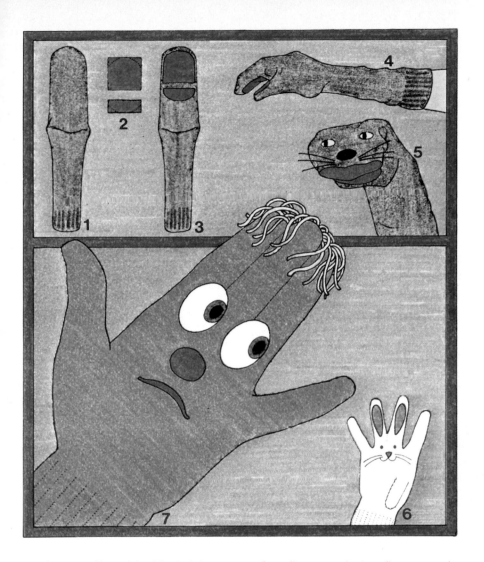

pipe cleaners dipped in black ink or painted black. Embroider any details you like in thread (5).

Variations Gloves also make delightful instant puppets. Glue pieces of felt to the palm for eyes, nose, and mouth. Sew lengths of yarn to the fingertips for hair. Use the little finger and the thumb for arms (7).

A sweet rabbit puppet can be made from a white glove. Glue felt to the fronts of two fingers. Embroider or draw in eyes, nose, and whiskers. Do not use the thumb. Work the puppet on four fingers only, two fingers working the ears, and the other two working the front legs (6).

Socks can also be used to make good puppet heads. Stuff the toe of a sock with cotton wool. Cut off the neck and tie it. You can embroider the stuffed toe with wool yarn or just sew on two bright beads for eyes.

You can make a long snake puppet by cutting the feet from a number of socks and joining the cut edges. Round off the last sock, and stitch to make a rounded head. Stuff the snake with other old socks and nylon tights.

Hand glove puppet

After you have experimented with glove-type puppets made from socks, mittens, paper bags, and boxes, you may want to progress to a proper hand glove puppet with sleeves. The thumb and little finger go through the sleeves and become the puppet's arms. The puppet head can be an old ball, or you can make a soft head from a circle of fabric like a piece of old nylon tights or the toe of a sock. The edge of the circle is gathered up with thread, pulled up to make a ball, and then stuffed with cotton wool. It is easy to push the middle finger into the gathered neck **(1)**. The features can either be painted on the head or embroidered with coloured threads.

Method for the basic glove A simple sleeveless glove is made by folding the piece of material across the middle, with the right sides together, and then sewing up the sides, stopping

about 40 mm from the fold **(2)**.

Cut a slit in the middle of the fold, 12 mm long. Snip outwards from the slit. This makes a hole with points round it **(3)**. Sew or glue the points to the neck of the puppet head **(4)**. Hem the sleeve openings to neaten.

Method for T-shaped glove Cut a piece of material 400 mm long × 150 mm wide. Fold it, right sides together. Pin it down the sides. Measure 25 mm in from the sides and 37 mm down from the fold. Pencil in lines. Sew on the pencilled lines. Cut the fabric away 6 mm from the stitching. Cut the star slits for the neck **(5)**.

Turn a neat hem on the sleeve ends.

Professional puppeteers sew a small ring to the hem of the glove so that they can hang puppets up when they are not using them **(6)**. They can also hang the puppets up backstage during a show so they can quickly slip a hand into the hanging puppet.

Cuffs and hands Separate sleeves can be sewn to the basic glove **(7)** and the ends left plain, or gathered on elastic. You can add lace or fur trims **(8)**. You can also sew up the sleeve ends and make tiny hands of felt, sewing them into the seam at the ends of the sleeves **(9)**.

Paper pulp heads

Heads for glove puppets, rod puppets and marionettes (string puppets), can be improvised from balls, food pots, and so on. To make permanent heads, model them from clay, or make them in paper pulp or paper strip. Paper pulp is made from newspaper and wallpaper paste. This makes the finished head hard and firm and it will last for a long time. Ordinary wallpaper paste is best for making paper pulp, but a flour and water paste can also be used.

Wallpaper paste method Tear newspaper into tiny pieces. Put a 25 mm deep layer into a bowl. Sprinkle on a thin layer of wallpaper paste powder. Tear up another 25 mm layer of paper and sprinkle on paste. Continue until the bowl is half-full of pressed-down layers. Pour in cold water (1). Stir to make a pulp ball (2). Leave for an hour before using.

Flour and water paste method Mix together 1 cup of plain flour, 3½ cups approximately of cold water, 1 tablespoon of salt. Stir water into flour and salt gradually so that there are no lumps. Pour into saucepan. Cook over low heat, stirring. Eventually the paste will go thick and clear. Tear up small pieces of paper and add to the warm paste until you have a paper pulp. It can be used immediately. The paper pulp is worked over a mould (3). The mould can either be left inside the finished head (balls for instance need not be removed) or the finished pulp head can be cut from the mould (4).

Necks A puppet head needs a neck whether it is a glove puppet or a marionette. In glove puppets, the neck is used for putting the middle or index finger into the head so that the head can be moved (6). The clothes are

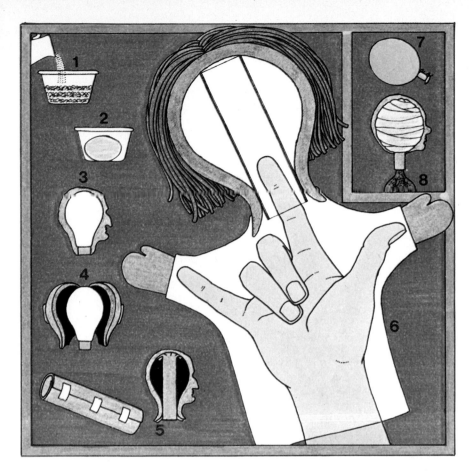

glued or sewn to the neck. Necks can be made from cardboard tubes, or you can make tubes by cutting pieces of card, rolling them up, and joining the seam with adhesive tape **(5)**.

Moulds Anything that is roughly the right size and shape will make a mould: balls, fruit such as oranges, lemons, and grapefruit, and some vegetables. Electric light bulbs make very good moulds, but you must be careful when working with them because they will shatter if you drop them. Balloons, blown up, with the neck tied tightly, make large puppet head moulds **(7)**.

Using the pulp Cover the surface of your mould with cooking oil. This helps to prevent the pulp from sticking to the mould. Stand the mould on a support of some kind, like a bowl or a jar. Apply a thin layer of pulp with your hands, spreading it over the surface. Leave it to dry. Turn the mould so that you can cover the rest of the surface with pulp. Build up the features, like the forehead, eyebrows, nose, and chin, by modelling the pulp with your fingers or with a matchstick.

After the pulp is dry, cut the head from the mould. Join the two halves of the head with pasted paper strips. Cut tabs in the end of the neck tube. Glue the tabs and push into the head **(5)**. You can also make a puppet head directly onto a cardboard tube, winding pasted paper strips round the tube first to make a rough shape and finishing with pulp **(8)**. Give finished heads a coat of emulsion paint before painting features.

Strip paper heads

Making puppets with the strip paper method gives you a finer finish than with pulped paper. This is important if you want to make detailed features. Ordinary newsprint should be used for the first six layers. Finish with two layers of soft tissue paper to give you a good painting surface.

Flour and hot water paste works quite well, but cellulose wallpaper paste makes a very strong head. A mould is used for the strip paper method, just as for paper pulp modelling. In the photograph only the puppet on the right is made from strip paper. The other is a paper pulp head.

Method for using a light bulb mould
Prepare the paste according to the instructions given on the paste box. Tear newspaper into small pieces, about 25 mm square, or 25 × 50 mm strips. The size of the pieces depends on the finished size of the head you are making. If the mould is going to be removed from the paper shell, cover the surface of the mould with cooking oil. Stand the mould on a jar or bottle to support it. Dip pieces of paper in the paste and apply them to the surface of the mould **(1)**. Cover the mould in this way with two layers of pasted paper. Leave to dry and apply two more. Leave to dry and apply two final layers. If you want to build up features, make some

paper pulp and build them on the surface between the second and final layers. The mould is laid on its side on the support for this stage. Fix the pulp to the head with paper strips pasted up the sides **(2)**.

When the head is quite dry, cut it from the mould with a craft knife **(3)**. Make a cardboard tube for the neck. Snip into one end of the tube and bend back the tabs **(4)**. Join the two halves of the head with strips pasted over the join **(5)**. Spread glue on the neck tube tabs and push into the head so that the tabs are against the top inside. Leave to dry. Pierce holes in the neck for fastening the head to a glove.

Variations A head can be modelled using modelling clay and then used as a mould for the paper strip method. The model should be very roughly shaped, as the detail is then built up in paper. Fruit, such as oranges, lemons,

and grapefruit, and vegetables, like turnips and carrots, can be used as moulds. Old tennis balls and rubber balls will make moulds and can be left inside the paper head afterwards. Cut a hole in the ball for the tube neck. You can also screw up a ball of paper for a mould, winding string round it to make it hold the shape **(6)**. A long head shape can be made with strips of cardboard wound and glued round a long tube. Paste strips over the tube to make the shape **(7)**.

Finishing Give the finished head a coat of white emulsion paint before painting. If doll's eyes or 'googlie' eyes are being used, make dents in the wet paper so that there is an indentation for gluing the eyes in when the head is finished. The head of the magician puppet illustrated was finished with strips of pink adhesive plaster. You could try this method on your puppets.

Spoon puppets

Rod puppets are a very old form of puppet. They can be simple, having just a head on a rod, or they can have moving arms and legs.

The simplest form of rod puppet, often used by professional puppeteers, is made from an ordinary wooden kitchen spoon. Spoon puppets seem almost too easy to make, but you will be surprised how effective they are when you use them.

All you need is a set of wooden spoons of different sizes, some paints, and some scraps of fabric for clothes.

Sand paper the bowl of the spoon first so that it is absolutely smooth. You can paint the wood with emulsion paint first to make it a flat colour before putting on the features, or you can work on the natural wood surface. Paint fairly bold features with exaggerated characters and expressions. The heads are small and you want to be sure that they can be seen and recognized by the people sitting at the back of the audience (1).

You can paint the same character on

the front and back of the spoon, giving it two expressions. One might be smiling and awake, and the reverse side fast asleep. Or you could have a laughing expression on one side and a crying face on the reverse **(2)**.

You can glue hair to the spoon puppets, long curly tresses, moustaches, beards, etc. You can give the female characters jewellery. Wire on tiny earrings and make small bead necklaces. Wooden spoon people look best in bright simple clothes.

Make robes by cutting out a circle of fabric with a tiny hole for the neck. Push the handle through the hole and draw it up to the neck. Tie or glue it to

the wood. You can also make a cloak or dress from a strip of fabric. Gather up one edge to tie round the neck of the spoon **(3)**.

Wooden spoon people can have arms made from pipe cleaners. Or, you can make paper arms and glue them to the inside of the robes, through slits in the fabric.

Animals can be made from wooden spoons. Make a paper or fabric body with hanging legs. Fold the body and hang it over the handle of the spoon. Make a string or felt tail. Make little ears. Paint the face on the bowl of the spoon **(4)**. Operate your spoon puppet by holding the end of the spoon.

Ghost rod puppet

Rod puppets are simple to make, but they can be made to move in many different ways, and given a lot of character. Some of the easiest, like the ghost rod puppet shown here, are the most effective.

Materials, tools, and equipment
Dowel or other wooden rod, 15-gauge wire
Fine white material
Paint, paste, glue, waterproof markers
Brushes, scissors, stapler, tenon saw, awl, pencil, ruler, rag, elastic bands, needle and thread
Trimmings for decoration

Method Take a 600 mm length of 12 mm dowel to be the rod. Make a head, about the same size as a tennis ball, using one of the methods given for glove puppets. Either the paper pulp head on pages 28–29, or the strip paper heads on pages 30–31 would work. Or, you could use an old ball, a box, or a tin. Add features by building up a nose, eyebrows, etc., with plastic wood or paper pulp. Make a hole or insert a tube to take the rod **(1)**.

Glue the rod into the head. When it is dry, paint with emulsion. Add features and hair.

To make the costume for the ghost puppet, take a piece of thin white material, such as old sheeting or net, 500 mm square. Mark a line 25 mm in along one side. On the edge of the material mark 12 mm in, and then 25 mm all along the edge. On the line down from edge mark 25 mm marks

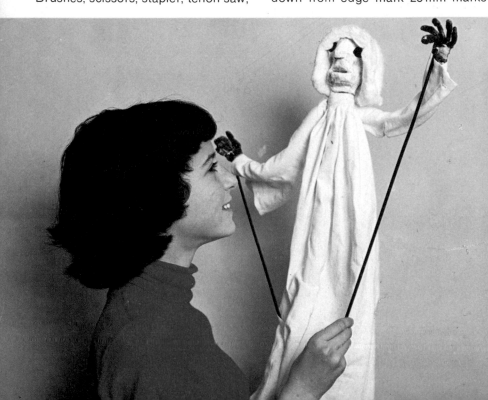

all along. Join up marks into a zigzag **(2)**. Cut on that dotted line. Gather this zigzag edge around under the head of your puppet. Glue into place, holding it with an elastic band until dry.

Make the neck by cutting a 25 × 100 mm strip of white material. Paste this around the neck. Use the elastic band again until dry **(3)**.

For arms, cut a strip of thin white material 325 × 62 mm, and fold in half lengthways. Stitch a straight line 6 mm in along the raw edge. Attach a large safety pin as shown **(4)**. Use safety pin to turn your tube inside out by pushing pin through tube. Remove pin. Mark centre of tube and draw two lines across, 37 mm each side of centre. Stitch over these two lines

and then stuff each arm with cotton wool.

Make hands by cutting out four hand shapes from white felt or thick material. Stick two shapes together to make one hand, trapping end of each sleeve inside **(5)**. When dry, paste the unstuffed part between the arms around the back of the neck. Fasten with a few stitches to the top of the costume at neck.

The two wire supports should each be about 600 mm long, and have 12 mm turned over at one end. This turn-over is sewn onto the palm of each hand.

You can now operate your puppet by moving the wire supports. See how many different ways you can make your ghost perform.

Rod and tube puppet

This type of rod puppet is similar to the basic rod puppet, but it has jointed limbs. The head is joined to a rod which is put inside a tube. This means that when the rod is pushed up from inside the tube, the head can appear to rise in the air on the neck, perhaps in surprise. The head can also be turned round to look in another direction.

Materials, tools, and equipment
Wooden ball for head, paint, false hair
Wood rod 90 cm long, wood dowelling for limbs
Cardboard tube a little shorter than the rod

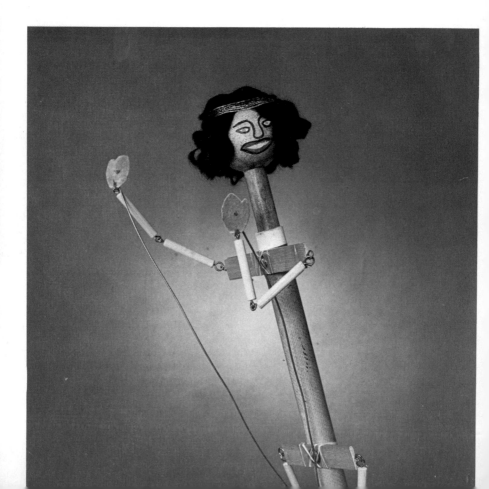

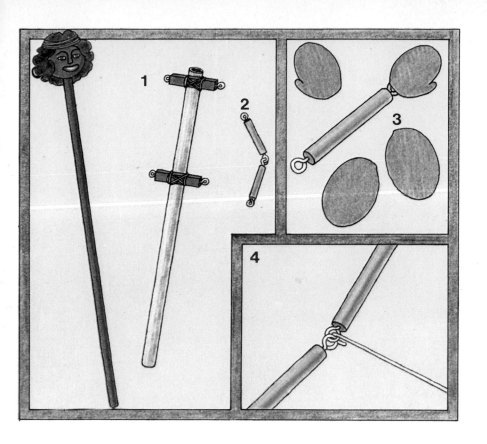

4 wire controls 60 cm long
2 shoulder and hip bars made from
   thin strips of wood 10 cm
   long × 25 mm wide
22 screw eyes, strong thread
Scraps of leather for hands and feet
Glue, adhesive tape, pliers

Method Glue the two cross-pieces
to the cardboard tube. Wind strong
thread round the join, and finish off
with adhesive tape. The shoulder
cross-piece is about 25 mm from the
top of the tube, and the hip cross-
piece 25 cm from the bottom of the
tube. Screw the screw eyes into the
ends of the cross-pieces **(1)**.

Make arms and legs in two pieces,
using the dowelling. Join limbs with
screw eyes. You will have to open out
one screw eye to join it to another,
and close it up again afterwards. Join
limbs to the ends of the cross-pieces

(2). Screw a screw eye into the ends
of the arms. Cut hand and foot
shapes, and glue to the ends of the
limbs **(3)**.

Cut the wire for the control rods.
Bend the ends and pass the controls
for the legs through one of the rings
at the knees. Bend the controls for
the arms through the rings at the
wrists **(4)**.

Push the rod, with the finished
head, through the tube.

Operating the rod puppet This is
rather a difficult puppet to operate
because you need both hands to
operate the control rods and yet the
puppet must be supported. The best
way to do this is to make yourself an
apron with a narrow, deep pocket.
Slip the end of the rod into the
pocket. This leaves your hands free to
operate the wire rods.

String witch rod puppet

This is another kind of rod puppet. The limbs are worked in a similar way to a marionette's, as they are pulled by strings. The puppet illustrated is made of card, and painted so that it can be used with a puppet theatre. You can make the puppet in stiff black card to be used with a shadow screen. Animal puppets can be made in the same way.

Materials, tools, and equipment
Thin strip of wood 102·5 cm long
  × 25 mm wide
3 screw eyes, tenon saw
Stiff cardboard, push-through paper
  fasteners (split pins), bradawl,
  woodworker's glue
Scissors or craft knife
Macramé thread, adhesive tape, panel
  pins, hammer

Method Plan the figure on paper first, marking in the joins and overlaps (as you did for the shadow puppet on pages 14–15) **(1)**. Draw the pieces on card. Mark holes for the joins. Paint the pieces if you want to.

Cut the pieces out. Pierce holes (2). Join pieces with split pins.

Making the rod Cut the main rod 90 cm long. Put in screw eyes, 12 mm, 150 mm, and 300 mm down from the top end on the main rod (3).

Fix the puppet to the main rod on the opposite side to the screw eyes. Do this by tapping in a panel pin on the point marked X on the figure (2) opposite the top screw eye (4).

Attach a 90 cm length of thread to the back of one hand, using a scrap of adhesive tape. Take the end of the thread up through the top screw eye, then down through the other screw eyes. Do the same with the other hand (5). If you prefer, pierce holes in the hands and tie the threads through the holes.

The puppet should swing easily on the rod, and from the hip joints. Hold the puppet in one hand and operate the strings with the other hand.

Jointed limb rod puppets

In this project two very exciting forms of rod puppet are described. Both puppets have joints, which means that they can move their limbs. Although the controls look difficult they are quite easily handled, and the audience probably won't even notice the wires.

Materials, tools, and equipment

Round dowel rod, screw eyes, 15-gauge wire

Paint, paste, waterproof markers, glue, thread

Brushes, scissors, tenon saw, awl, pliers, needle

Trimmings for decoration and costume

Method for jointed shoulder bar puppet Take a 90 cm length of 12 mm diameter round dowel for the main rod of your puppet. Glue one end of this rod into a hole in a head. This head should be about tennis ball size. It can be made from an old ball, or by one of the methods previously described, such as the paper pulp or strip paper techniques. Allow a space for the neck. Cut a V-shaped nick below the neck to take the shoulder bar. The shoulder bar is a 125 mm length of dowel 12 mm diameter. Glue this to the nick on the main rod, hold with a clamp or clip until dry **(1)**. Make a hole in each end of this shoulder bar with an awl or gimlet to take a screw eye.

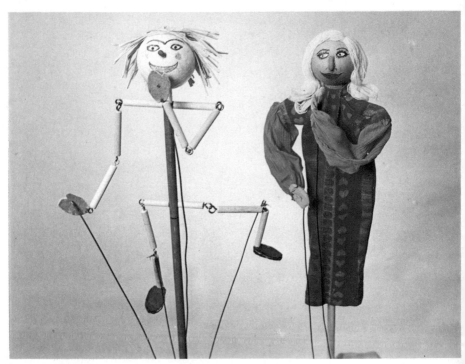

Each arm is made from two pieces of dowel rod each 62 mm long. Make holes in each end and insert screw eyes. Open out one screw eye on each piece. Join up the shoulder joints, and elbow joints, and close up the screw eyes.

Make the hands from two pieces of card or felt cut out to shape. Stick them together and sew on to the screw eye at the wrist.

Attach the wire supports, each 75 cm long, to the centre of each hand. Push the wire through the hand, bend the wire back 6 mm and stick or sew to the back of the hand **(2)**.

You are now ready to draw on features with markers or paint. Use rug wool, frayed string, cotton wool, raffia, etc., for hair, beards, and moustaches. Wire makes good spectacles. Model the nose, eyebrows, etc., with scraps of wood or modelling clay. Finally make a loose costume to dress your puppet.

Method for double-joint bar puppet
Make a puppet in the way described for the shoulder bar puppet, and then make a second shoulder bar and arms unit, 75 mm wide. Attach this to your main rod by making a nick 200 mm down from the top of the head. Stick in place as for shoulders to make a hip bar **(3)**. Add feet, shoes or boots, and then decorate your puppet.

Connect the wires for the legs just above the knee joint by making a hole and pushing the wire through. Bend an end of the wire over at the back and the rest of the wire should come down in front. The wire should move freely in the hole.

At first you may find it difficult to control four wires. Practice will help, or you may get a friend to help, or you can wear a belt with a small pocket in front. Put the bottom of the main rod in the pocket. This leaves two hands free to operate the controls **(4)**.

Simple fabric marionettes

Marionettes are puppets controlled by strings which are fastened to different parts of the figure. The strings are pulled from above the marionette to make the head and limbs move. Some marionettes have just one or two strings, while others can have strings fastened to head, shoulders, elbows, wrists, hips, knees and ankles.

The easiest of all marionette-type puppets to make uses only two things, a square of thin material and some thread.

Materials, tools, and equipment
A square of thin material, gauze, nylon, chiffon, etc.
Macramé thread or button thread.

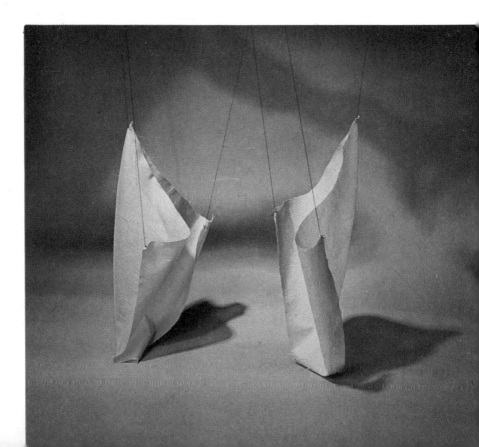

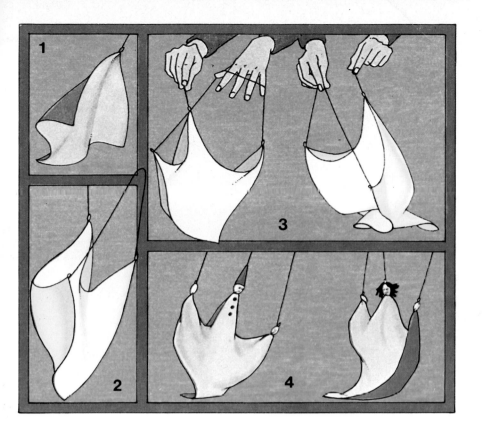

Method You can cut the fabric to any size of square you like, but a 30 cm square is big enough. Cut a long length of thread and tie it to one corner **(1)**. Cut a second long length of thread and tie each end to two opposite corners as in **(2)**. To operate the puppet, hold the top thread by the end until the opposite corner just touches the table. Hold the 'bridle' fastened to the other corners in the other hand, and practise 'walking' the handkerchief across the table top. You will see that it moves rather like a little ghost. The arms wave and float, and the tail just drifts across the table. You can make it wave its arms, run across the table, turn round, sit down. Make a second puppet in the same way and practise with a friend **(3)**. See if you can make the puppets bow to one another, play leap frog, walk side by side. Perhaps one could lie down

and sleep and the other try to wake it up. By getting used to doing all kinds of things with this simple thread control, you will be getting practice operating marionettes with more complex controls.

To make more realistic-looking marionettes, you could tie knots in the squares for heads and hands. You can paint faces on the handkerchiefs, or even make small accessories out of paper **(4)**.

You can have a lot of fun with two ghosts made out of flimsy white fabric. Paint a set to look like a gloomy churchyard with dark, racing clouds above and a pale moon. Paint gravestones on the backdrop. Make side sets of black bushes. Make a tomb and then, to ghostly music, bring the ghosts out of the tomb slowly and make them perform a weird and mournful dance.

Animal card marionette

This is your first project in stringing a marionette. Strings are fastened to parts of the puppet so that when the different strings are pulled, parts of the marionette move. On a simple flat card marionette like the lion illustrated, you only need three strings, one to operate the big head and two simply to support the body.

Materials, tools, and equipment
Stiff cardboard
Thick, hairy string for tail
Paints and felt-tipped pens
Scissors, sharp craft knife, adhesive tape, bradawl
Macramé thread, split pins
Half a wooden coat-hanger
Two small screw eyes
One large screw eye
Tracing paper, pencil and ruler

Method The graph pattern (1) shows the shapes you need to make the lion. Copy them onto squared paper. The scale is 1 square to 25 mm. A is the head, B the body, C is the back legs, D the front legs. Trace the pieces. Rub soft pencil over the back of your tracing paper and then draw over the lines on white card. Cut the shapes out carefully. You need two of the leg shape C.

Colour the pieces boldly. The black

dots on the pattern are where you make holes with a bradawl for the split pin fasteners. Put the two back legs on first, one each side of the body **(2)**. Put the front legs section on next and then the head on top of the front legs. The legs should swing easily, so do not put the split pin fasteners in too tightly. Screw three screw eyes into the half coat-hanger. This makes the control bar **(3)**. Lay the lion face down on the table. Glue on a piece of string for a tail. Cut a long piece of thread for the lion's head control. Tape it to the back of the head in two places, taking the thread through the first screw eye on the control bar **(4)**. Fasten the second thread to the back of the lion's front body. Take the thread end and tie to the second screw eye. The last thread is attached to the back of the lion's body and is tied to the third screw eye **(5)**.

Stand the lion on his feet, holding the control bar, and see that all the threads are the right length so that he stands easily. Practise lifting the threads with your fingertips as you hold the control to make the lion's head move. Screw the large screw eye into the top of the control as a hanger for the puppet **(6)**.

When you are operating the puppet, try not to let the control be seen by the audience.

Junk
marionettes

A simple marionette made from cotton reels will help you to understand how a marionette is strung. Keep this type of puppet very simple when you

make the clothes. Half of the charm lies in the fact that it is made from cotton reels.

Materials, tools, and equipment
3 ordinary cotton reels, 4 long, thin
    cotton reels, thin twine, washers
Scraps of leather or cardboard
Screw eyes, adhesive, fabric tape,
    beads

Method   Use a large cotton reel or a polystyrene ball for the head. Knot the end of a piece of thin twine. Pass through the cotton reel. Secure the knot with a spot of glue. Slide a few washers up the string to make a neck **(1)**. Add two more cotton reels for the body. Slide on two more washers in between them at the waist, knotting the string underneath them. Tie on

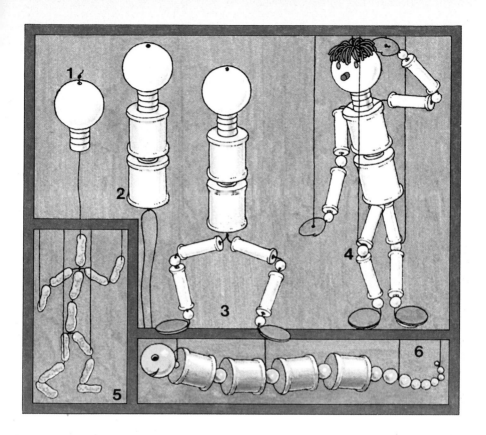

lengths of twine for the legs **(2)**. Thread long, narrow cotton reels on the leg strings, with a bead between each reel for the knee and ankle joints **(3)**.

Make big floppy feet from paper strip or plastic wood. Cover these with plastic-surfaced tape. Make the hands from scraps of leather or from cardboard. Make the arms in the same way as the legs.

Attach the control threads to the top of the head through a screw eye. Attach another control thread in the same way to the end of each hand and another in between the beads at each of the knees **(4)**. Cover the neck washers with a strip of adhesive fabric tape.

Variations You can make a peanut puppet at the next party you go to where they serve peanuts in their shells. You need some macrame thread, and a long, strong needle. Start with the head and two long threads. Pass the threads through the peanut, on the needle. Tie the ends with a knot. Take the thread ends through peanuts to make arms, and back to the centre of the figure for the body. Pass both threads through the two body peanuts. Separate the strands to make two legs. Thread the leg peanuts and then take the needle back up through the nuts to the hips. Knot the thread ends off **(5)**.

Cotton reel caterpillar Use two threads and string through the cotton reels and beads, to the tail. Take the thread round one bead and then thread back through all the beads and reels to the head **(6)**.

Cone clown marionette

Here is another way of making a puppet from odds and ends of paper and card. It is a development of the flat card puppets. The paper is made into cones so that the body is three-dimensional. You can practise stringing the puppet onto a crossbar control before you go on to make more complicated marionettes.

Materials, tools, and equipment
Medium thick paper or thin card
Glue, adhesive tape, compass, beads
Macramé thread, fishing line or
    strong button thread
Scrap of tissue for hat decoration

Method Draw three circles on the

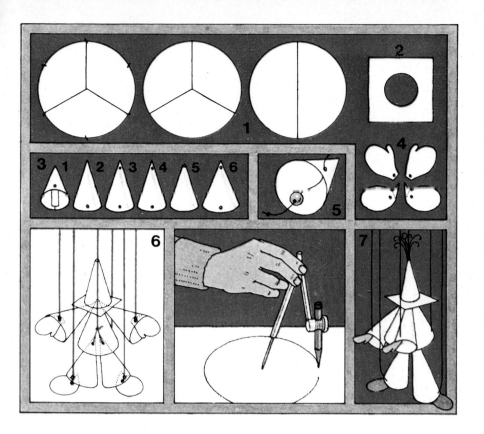

paper, radius 37 mm. Still using the compass, mark off this same measurement round the circumference of the circles. Mark off sections 1, 2, 3, 4, 5, 6 as shown (1). Sections 1–5 make cones for the arms, legs, and head. Section 6 is the body cone. Cut out a square of paper 50 mm square. In the centre (2), cut out a circle 25 mm across. Roll cones 1–5 and glue the join or use sticky tape. Cut the tip off cone 5. Roll cone 6 for the body. Pierce holes in the cone for stringing (3).

Cut out hand and feet shapes. Pierce holes for stringing (4).

The strings have beads tied to the end to help to weight the puppet. Tie a knot in the end of each string, pass through a bead and then through a hole in the cone (5).

Follow drawing (6) for the method used to string the puppet. String the feet first, then the beads for the cone legs, numbers 3 and 4. Put another string through the tops of the leg cones. Knot the two threads together and cut one end off. Take the remaining thread through cone 6, put on the square collar and then go through the head cone, number 5. String the hands and then take the string through arm cones 1 and 2. Flatten the pointed ends of the cones and glue to the sides of the body. Cut a fringe of tissue for the decoration on the top of the clown's hat.

Attach a separate string to the hole at the edge of the body cone (7).

If you like, you could use coloured paper for the clown's body cones, with a plain paper cone for the head. Then you could paint a face on the cone for a realistic-looking puppet.

49

Newspaper marionette

This project shows you how an effective marionette can be made using just the simplest of materials. All you need is newspaper, paste, tape, and paint. The puppet illustrated has a head made of paper pulp and paper strip over a newspaper base. The hands are covered with pink adhesive plaster, and the boots with black adhesive tape.

Materials, tools, and equipment
Quantity of newspaper, lead weights
3 m white tape 12 mm wide, macramé thread
Wallpaper paste, large bead, clear adhesive, bradawl

Method To make the head, cut 750 mm tape and fold. Tie 30 mm length of thread onto the fold. Fold half of a large-size newspaper page to make a folded strip about 300 × 75 mm **(1)**. Paste this around the tape just under the knot. Leave the threads hanging out. About 200 mm of tape ends will hang down. Hold the newspaper together with rubber bands until dry **(2)**.

Fold another half-page to make a strip about 150 × 37 mm and paste this over the top of the head, leaving the threads hanging **(3)**. Build up the

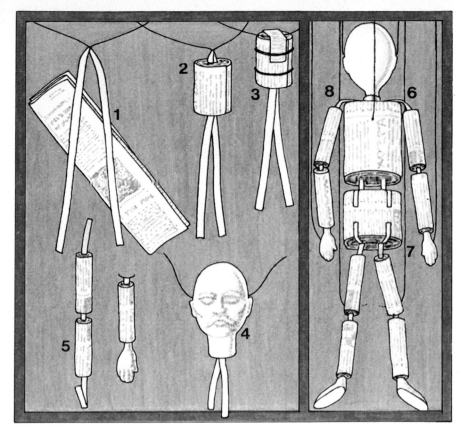

head and neck with paper strips and use pulp to make the features. Leave thread coming out at ear positions and tapes hanging out below neck **(4)**.

Arms and legs Cut four lengths of tape 300 mm long. Fold each length of tape. Tear eight strips of paper each 300 mm long × 75 mm wide. Fold and paste the newspaper strips round the tape. Each strip makes half of a limb. Leave 12 mm of tape uncovered for elbow and knee joints **(5)**. For arms, fold one end of tape in half and tie 150 mm of thread round the fold. Use pasted paper scraps to build up the hand shape round the tape. Leave the thread hanging. Put a tiny piece of lead inside the hand to weight it, if you can obtain lead. For the legs, fold paper over the tape, including the feet. Weight each foot.

Upper body Fold two or three pieces of newspaper for the body as you did for the head. Wrap it round a ruler, pasting as you wrap. Take out the ruler.

Lower body Make in the same way as the upper body, using a ruler, but make this section a little smaller.

Assembling the puppet Thread the head tapes through a large bead and then through the upper body **(6)**. Thread the leg tapes up through the lower body, leaving 12 mm between the top of the legs and the body **(7)**. Take them over the top and glue down the back of the lower body.

Glue loose ends of arm tapes into slits on top of shoulders, leaving 12 mm of tape free for shoulder joint **(8)**. Use a bradawl to make a hole in the upper legs to tie the thread through. Paint the head. Dress the puppet as required.

Stringing a marionette

Marionettes are probably the most difficult puppets to make and operate. Their advantage is that they seem to move freely in space. If you practise the basic movements you will soon be able to operate your puppet well. This section shows you how to make a balanced control for your marionette.

Materials, tools, and equipment
Wood laths (smooth, thin strips of soft wood like deal) approximately 20 × 6 mm

Fabric (for clothes), small pieces of lead
Screw eyes, 15-gauge wire, elastic, nails, pins, macramé thread or fine fishing line, large and small cup hooks, large bulldog clips, rag
Scissors, stapler, awl, hammer, pincers, pliers, paint brushes
Glue, paste, paint, polyurethane varnish

Method for stringing The controls described are in order of difficulty in making and use. The following key has been used for naming the strings.
A – Arm. Strings consist of a loop or running string which passes through one or two screw eyes on the control. They are attached through a hole in the centre of each puppet's hands, and tied round the hand.
B – Back. A wire joined to shoulders and down the back of the body, or a string joined to just below the waist.
BL – Back legs for animals.
FL – Front legs for animals.
H – Head. The first string to be attached. It is fastened to the top of the head. When two strings are used, attach one to a screw eye behind each ear.
L – Legs. Usually a free-running loop, best tied above the knee joint.
Sh – Shoulders.
T – Tail for animals.
   In all the diagrams the working strings are shown in red to make them different from construction strings or joins. Strings are usually white, black, natural, or transparent.

Method for single-bar control This control consists of a straight piece of

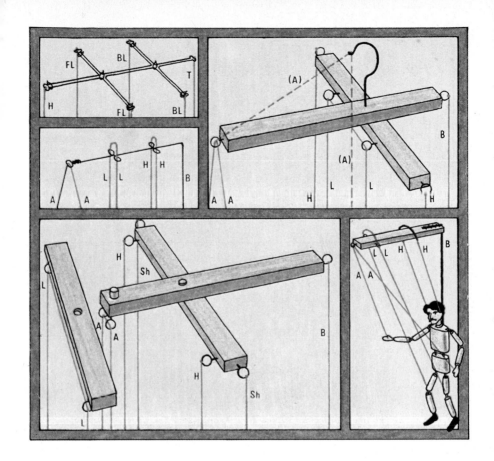

wood about 300 × 25 × 12 mm with screw eyes and strings, a piece of stiff wire and 150 mm of elastic **(1)**. The stiff wire (B) is glued and stapled at the back of the wood control, and to the back (not head) of the puppet. The macramé thread used for the strings runs freely through the screw eyes, except for the head strings (H). These do not go through screw eyes. They have a short piece of elastic which goes over the control to give realistic head movements.

Method for aeroplane control This control is suitable for puppets up to 300 mm in height **(2)**. It consists of two pieces of wood each 300 × 25 × 12 mm. The cross-bar pivots on the hook to make it easier

to pack away. The hook is made of stiff wire and can be fixed by bending back under the main bar.

The strings are of two types. Those for the head (H), and back (B) are fixed. The others for legs (L), and arms (A) are continuous run-through strings. If necessary the arm string (A) can be pulled up to the top hook (see dotted line in diagram). The continuous string allows either the legs or arms to be lifted or dropped singly, together or alternately without having to change strings.

The control is held in one hand, and the other hand is used for individual strings. By tipping the control forwards the puppet will bow. Tipping it from side to side it will shake its head.

Carved wood marionette

Some of the marvellous marionettes used by famous puppeteers were made entirely from wood. The arms were either soft, made in the same way as the ghost rod puppet (on pages 34–35), or they were carved from wood and jointed. Wooden marionettes will not wear out easily, so it is worth making costumes for them which can be taken off and put on for changes of character. The wood puppet illustrated is the easiest method of making a puppet out of wood. If you enjoy carving, you can shape the head block to give it features, or you can build up a nose and forehead with plastic wood.

This puppet is simple to make and uses dowelling for the arms and legs, and pieces of leather cut from an old glove for hands and feet.

Materials, tools, and equipment
Softwood 225 × 50 × 25 mm
Wood dowel 500 × 12 mm diameter
21 screw eyes, pliers for opening
   screw eyes, tenon saw, bradawl,
   Surform tool
Sand paper, white emulsion paint,
   modeller's enamel paints, glue
Doll's hair, fabric for clothes
Wood control, macramé thread

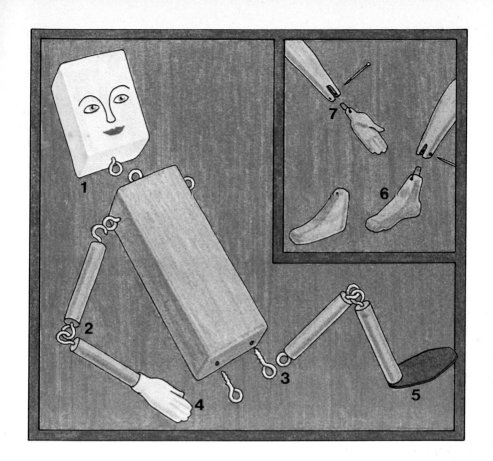

Method Cut the head piece 75 mm long. Cut the body piece 150 mm long. Round off all edges with the Surform tool and sand smooth. Make holes in the head piece and the body and put in screw eyes for joining head to body, and for attaching the arms and legs. Open one screw eye and join the head to the body **(1)**.

Paint the puppet's features in now. If you are building up features with plastic wood, the modelling should be finished and the painting done before you go any further.

Cut the dowelling into eight pieces, each 60 mm long. Make holes at each end of four pieces. Make holes at one end of each of the remaining four pieces. Join one of each to make two arms and two legs **(2)**. Screw an eye to the end of the arms and at the ankles for the thread controls **(3)**. Open

screw eyes and join legs to the underbody, and arms to the body near to the shoulders. Cut hands from leather and glue to the ends of the arms **(4)**. Cut feet from leather and glue to the ends of the legs **(5)**.

Modelled legs, feet, and hands The legs of the puppet illustrated are straight lengths of dowelling, but you could use thicker dowelling and carve curves in the legs. You can also make feet and hands from plastic wood, modelling it over small pieces of lead sheet. Put in small loops of wire as you model **(6)**. Fix hands and feet to the ends of shaped wrists and ankles with panel pins **(7)**.

To string the puppet after dressing Tie strings to screw eyes at wrist, ankle, and top of the head. Glue on hair.

Soft face witch marionette

This puppet uses another method for making heads. The head is made of fabric, drawn up with threads to make the features. The body is very simple, just dowelling and padding. It can be given a very realistic-looking face, depending on the way in which the stuffing and sewing is done.

Materials, tools, and equipment
Nylon tights or stockings
Stuffing, cotton wool, kapok,
    shredded nylon tights, foam chips
Plastic wood, wood dowelling, lead
    weights
Screw eyes, tenon saw, bradawl
Needle and thread, scissors, fabric for
    clothes

Method for making the head
Stretch out a stocking or one leg of a pair of tights. Stuff the toe with cotton wool or other filling. Tie firmly underneath to make a ball **(1)**. Thread the needle and tie a knot at the end.

Start in the middle of the face and draw up the fabric to make the nose. Draw the threads up tightly, picking up some of the stuffing with the fabric **(2)**. Aim to give character to the face by the way in which you pull up the fabric with stitches.

Glue on hair and add any other trims to the face **(3)**. Embroider outline of eyes in silk threads.

To make the neck, cut a piece from a cardboard tube and push up inside the stocking under the stuffed head. Tie under the tube with thread.

Cut a piece of wood dowelling for the shoulder bar and push through the stocking, right up under the neck. Fasten in position by binding thread

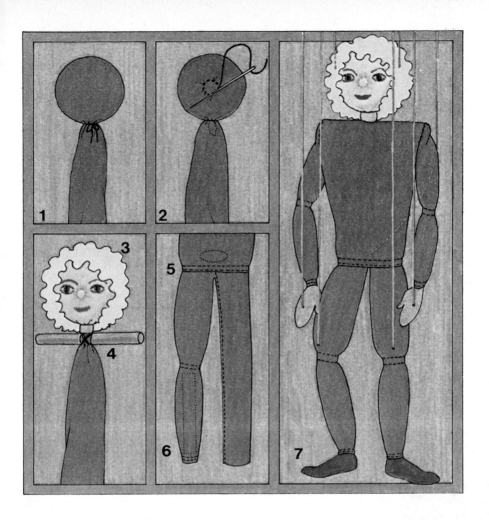

round (**4**). Stuff the rest of the body down to the waist with cotton wool. Pad around the shoulder bar, shaping the body into a wedge shape. Continue stuffing down the body, putting in scraps of lead weight to give the body some weight when it is strung. Wrap the leads in cotton wool so that they do not move around.

Legs and feet   Double stitch the bottom of the stocking to make legs. Cut up between the legs, leaving 6 mm seams. Double stitch across the top of the legs (**5**). This has made two long tubes. Stuff the legs with cotton wool, pushing it in with a pencil. Double stitch to make a knee joint.

Push a piece of wood dowel into the lower leg (**6**). Pad around the wood dowel. Double stitch to the ankle.

Cut off any surplus stocking leg and sew on the feet.

Arms and hands   Make the arms from tubes of stocking. Stuff them, and put dowelling in the lower part of the arms. Sew the arms and legs firmly to the stuffed body, stitching joins at the elbows and the wrists. Weight the hands and sew on the arms. These can be made from balsa wood, wood filler modelled over pieces of lead, or shaped using adhesive fabric tape. Attach the strings as shown in diagram (**7**).

Materials, tools, and equipment
Shoe box or one of similar size
Paper, card, cellophane, sweet
   wrappings, acetate, tissue paper
All-purpose adhesive, sticky tape

Peepshow

Before you make a model theatre, try making a peepshow in a cardboard box. You can use this in lots of ways. The actors and scenery can be static and not move at all, or you can glue actors onto rods and move them on and off stage through holes in the sides of the box. The backdrop scenery can also be changed, by making slits in the sides of the box end. The scene changes are pushed on and off through the slits.

Method At one end of the box, measure the depth and then the width to find the middle. Cut a small round hole. If you can find a piece of cardboard tube, glue it into the hole to make a peephole **(1)**. Decide on a theme for the peepshow. It should be something which gives you a chance to make exciting scenery like a treasure island, a moon landscape, a desert, or a jungle. The scene illustrated is the old Wild West of America. Plan how you will make the scenery as 'flats'. Flats go at the sides of a stage. Remember that the flat nearest the front must have more cut away than the flat at the back, otherwise the front flats will hide the back flats. The peepshow illustrated has four flats **(2)**.

To make a flat, measure the width of the box and add 25 mm for side

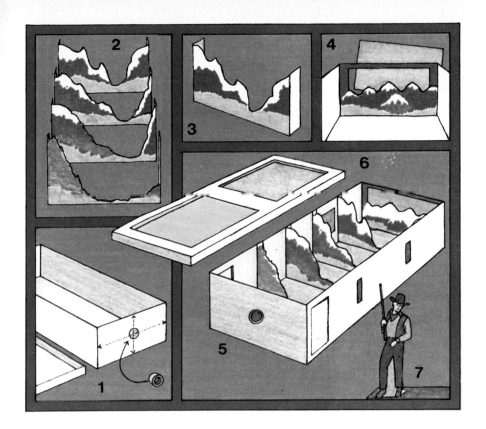

tabs. Flats can be any depth, but not deeper than the box. Fold back the tabs and paint the flats (3).

Look through the peephole and decide where you will place your figures.

Draw the back scenery on the inside of the box at the end. The peepshow illustrated has a mountain range. Cut out a mountain, and then glue a piece of blue acetate or cellophane on the outside of the box behind the mountain (4).

Cut two doors at the front end of the box at the sides. Cut slits 50 mm high at the sides of the box where you need to get your actors and animals on and off the stage. Cut small windows where you want your stage lighting. You can test this by putting the lid on the box, and seeing where you need lighting effects. The peepshow illustrated has a small window on the left-hand side with pink cellophane glued to it so that

the light on this side makes a pink glow on the actors. Now you can glue the flats in position (5). Paint the side walls if you like.

Add small pieces of greenery for trees at the sides of the stage. Brush glue on the floor and sprinkle sand and small stones.

Making the lid For the western stage set, light is needed on the mountains at the back of the stage and a different light in the foreground. Cut parts of the lid away at each end and glue coloured cellophane to give overhead light (6).

Figures You can use model toys if you like, or you can cut actors and animals from pictures in magazines and comics. Cut strips of card about 150 mm long and 6 mm wide. Glue the figures to the ends of the strips (7). Push them on stage through the side slits.

Push-on theatre

Push-on puppet shows, using a minia-ture theatre, are very old and were very popular right up to the 19th century. You can make a theatre like the one illustrated and act out a play with friends, reading from a script. You will have more of a chance to use scenery than with a peepshow, and you can create lighting effects, using torches or desk lamps.

Materials, tools, and equipment
Corrugated cardboard box 150 mm deep with top 225 × 312 mm
Wood battens, 2 pieces 300 mm long, 3 pieces 212 mm long, contact adhesive, sticky backed tape
Sharp craft knife, pencil, ruler, scissors
Brown or fawn paper
Heavy-weight cardboard for proscenium 50 × 69 cm
Art paper, paints, brush

Method Glue the battens to the bot-tom of the box to strengthen the stage. Mark and then cut out the

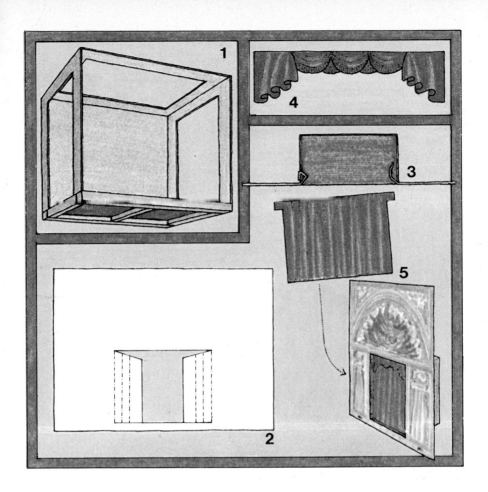

sides and top of the box leaving a margin all round the edges. Make the side and front cut-outs level with stage **(1)**. If there are flaps on the box, cut these off.

Cut a piece of plain coloured paper, brown or fawn, and stick to the floor of the stage. You are now ready to make the proscenium – the front of the stage.

On the heavy-weight cardboard draw a stage front 225 × 300 mm, 25 mm up from the bottom edge. Mark out the stage front. Draw two lines 25 mm in from each side and then a further line 37 mm in. From points 25 mm down from the top of the last two lines, draw short lines to each top corner **(2)**.

With a sharp knife and a piece of scrap cutting board underneath, cut along the solid lines and half-cut (score) along the dotted lines. Fold the flaps back carefully **(3)**.

Paint the proscenium if you like. When the paint is dry, glue the stage front onto the front of the box. You may have to use a strip of sticky tape to hold the flaps back.

Draw and paint curtain swags on paper. Glue them along the top of the stage **(4)**.

If you want to make a curtain that drops, paint a piece of thin card or stiff paper to look like curtains. Tape it to the back of the proscenium. Untape the curtain at the end of the scene and drop it down. The tabs at the side **(5)** rest on the side bars of the stage top.

Push-on scenery and animals

Many of the puppets described in previous projects may be used, or adapted for use, in the push-on stage. You can also make the push-on animals described on this page. There is plenty of opportunity for trying different sets, and using backcloths, and side flats. You will need similar materials, tools, and equipment to those used for making the theatre.

Method for making the scenery To make the backcloth, use a 337 mm wide × 250 mm high piece of thick card or hardboard **(1)**. Make the main centre part (marked A on diagram **(1)**) fit within the 288 mm width at the top of your stage. This means you can slide the backcloth up and down to change sets. The side tabs rest on top of the side top rails of the stage. The scenery can be painted directly onto the backcloth, which has been primed with white emulsion paint.

Alternatively you could use coloured pictures from magazines, newspaper supplements and cards.

The side flats or wings are either made to hang from the side, top rails of the stage with a small block of wood at base to steady the flat on the stage **(2)**, or suspended from a strip of wood resting across the top of the stage **(3)**. Small pieces of scenery, or props, are stuck to a strip of square wood **(4)**.

Method for making push-on puppets
The simplest type is made from figures or animals cut out from magazines or other illustrations. Glue these to thin card before cutting out. Stick the cutout onto a strip of square wood. Glue a length of dowelling to the back **(5)**. This is used to move your figures about the stage. Use smaller figures in the background to give distance to your stage. You can, of course, draw, colour and cut out your own figures.

Method for making walking push-on puppets Animals and figures with moving legs can be made. Cut two circles of card. Cut 5 legs into the circles. Make holes in the middle **(6)**.

Two split pin fasteners are glued to the back of the body **(7)**. The leg discs are placed on the fasteners so they turn round easily when the puppet is moved along by a hand rod as shown in **(8)**.

Birds and other flying creatures, or aeroplanes, space ships, rockets, etc., can be suspended by thread from a control bar resting across the top rails of the stage. They can be moved about the stage as required.

Music and sound effects help any performance. Sound effects are very simply produced. The rumble and crack of thunder can be reproduced by shaking a large sheet of tin or aluminium. The sound of rain is produced by rattling dried peas over a piece of metal mesh or hardboard.

Conversion table	
millimetres (mm)	inches (in)
3	⅛
6	¼
13	½
19	¾
25	1
38	1½
44	1¾
51	2
64	2½
76	3
89	3½
102	4
127	5
152	6
178	7
203	8
229	9
254	10
381	15
508	20
635	25
762	30
889	35

The photograph on page 7 is by courtesy of Museum of Mankind.